KU-526-267

Contents

Hadrian's Wall

Kings and Queens
of Scotland

W. A. Ross

Appletree Press

First published in 1997 by
The Appletree Press Ltd,
19-21 Alfred Street,
Belfast BT2 8DL.
Tel: +44 232 243074
Fax: +44 232 246756

Kings and Queens of Scotland

A catalogue record for this book is
available from the British Library.

ISBN 0 86281 626 2

9 8 7 6 5 4 3 2 1

1

The Origins of the Kingdom

Scotland is first mentioned in history in the first century AD, as Caledonia, with the arrival of the Romans. They found it a wild land of trackless forest, bog and mountain, where wolf and wild boar roamed and preyed on the deer. The human population was a group of hostile and uncivilised Celtic tribes, each in its own territory. The Romans' efforts at conquest failed, and resulted in the building of Hadrian's and Antonine's Walls to keep the barbarians out. North of the Roman walls, the tattooed and warlike tribesmen kept up their Iron Age lifestyle. They were not cut off from the world around; there were alliances with, and invasions from, Ireland to the west, England to the south, and Scandinavia to the north-east. And long after the Romans had gone, the numerous high chiefs and petty kings, remembering the power and prestige of the Roman Emperor, had their own titles styled in somewhat erratic Latin.

Eventually four distinct kingdoms emerged: Pictland in the

north, Dalriada in the west (the people there were named Scots, and this name was gradually adopted throughout the country), Strathclyde in the south-west, and Lothian in the south-east. In the Celtic kingdoms, the eldest son did not usually inherit. Succession was normally through the female line: the son of a king's sister could be nominated as the next king. This practice, known as tanistry, prevented weakling or child-kings in an age when the king's role as law-giver and war-leader was essential. But it promoted murder and blood-feuds among rival cousins. Royal families, once established, were considered as a breed apart; a king of Pictish origins might reign over the Scots, and vice versa.

A vigorous dynasty was founded in the ninth century by Kenneth McAlpin, king of the Scots who also, by a combination of violence and diplomacy, became king of the Picts in 843. It is possible that his mother was Pictish, but he could also trace his father's ancestry back to Fergus Mor who had led the Scots across the sea from Ireland over three centuries before. Kenneth was far the most powerful king in the north of Britain, and his overlordship was maintained by his descendants. The kings who were later to rule all Scotland numbered themselves from him.

At this time, there was neither a Scotland nor an England: the kingdom of Strathclyde reached south into Cumbria, and the kingdom of Lothian was often under English lordship. In 971, Edgar, king of most of England, ceded Lothian to the king of

Scots, who thus established control over the south-east, as far as the River Tweed. On the death in 1034 of Malcolm II, king of Scots, Picts and Lothian, his grandson Duncan, who was already king of Strathclyde, inherited the other king ships too. He was the first king of what came to be called Scotland. But huge tracts of Pictland had by then been overrun and settled by Vikings; and the Northern and Western Isles, and Caithness and Sutherland on the mainland, were ruled by Norse earls in the name of the king of Norway.

The island of Iona, burial place of the early Scottish kings

Shakespeare's Macbeth and the historical figure were very different

2

The Celtic and Norman-Celtic Kings

DUNCAN *(born c. 1001, reigned 1034-40)*
Duncan has become famous through drama as the murdered king in Shakespeare's *Macbeth*. He was an active and energetic king, or he would never have achieved and maintained a unified rule. But there must have been many traditionally-minded chiefs who resented Duncan's supremacy and wanted the old order restored, and it was not a peaceful reign. Duncan was not yet forty when he was killed, probably in battle, fighting his kinsman and rival Macbeth, Mormaer (earl) of Moray.

MACBETH *(born c. 1005, reigned 1040-57)*
The historical Macbeth was a very different figure from the Shakespearean one. He had a respectable claim to the throne, and ruled ably for seventeen years, while the sons of Duncan went into exile. He and his wife, Gruoch, appear to have been sincerely religious and his position was secure enough for them

to go on a pilgrimage to Rome. Northern Europe was in turmoil, with the power of the Normans about to culminate in their conquest of England. As Duncan's sons grew up, they sought to retrieve their father's throne, and Malcolm, the elder, invaded Scotland with the support of Earl Siward of Northumbria. Macbeth was defeated, very likely at Dunsinane, and was killed in a further battle shortly afterwards at Lumphanan, west of Aberdeen.

MALCOLM III *(born c. 1031, reigned 1058-93)*

Known as Canmore (from the Gaelic *ceann mor* meaning great head). An attempt was made to set up Macbeth's stepson, Lulach, as king, but Malcolm had him rapidly despatched. Despite English support in gaining his throne, he was an aggressive neighbour. His raids brought William I of England up into Scotland with an army and Malcolm had to pay homage in 1072, a bad omen for his successors. Raiding across the ill-defined Border nevertheless continued.

Malcolm's second wife was a remarkable woman, the only non-reigning queen to have a significant impact on the country. Margaret, an Anglo-Saxon princess, bore eight children, three of whom became Scottish kings. She brought new standards of culture and taste to the rough court. She was ignorant of and hostile to the Gaelic culture of Scotland, and abhorred the wayward tendencies of the Celtic Church. This reforming and modernising queen, Scotland's only royal saint (canonised in 1250) wanted the country to conform to the pattern of the European states she knew. She is remembered by St Margaret's Chapel in Edinburgh Castle, and by Queensferry on the Firth of Forth.

DONALD BAN *(born c. 1033, reigned 1093-4 and 1094-7, died 1099)* and DUNCAN II *(born c. 1061, reigned briefly 1094)*
Although Norman influence on the Scottish court was strong, there was still no automatic right of successsion by the eldest son. When Malcolm Canmore was killed on a raid into Cumberland, his brother sped from the Western Isles to assume the kingship. For four turbulent years, Donald Ban tried to turn St Margaret's clock back and reinstate a Gaelic kingdom. In 1094 King William Rufus of England produced a rival in the person of Duncan, son of Canmore by his first wife. This

Donald Ban's royal birlinn, or galley

Edinburgh Castle

Duncan was placed on the throne by English arms, and reigned for six months before Donald Ban and his nephew Edmund had him killed. But Donald was finally deposed by Edmund's younger brother Edgar, again with English help, in 1097. He was caught and blinded, and died two years later. He is the last king to be buried on Iona, and his descendants maintained a claim to the throne into the 13th century.

EDGAR *(born c. 1074, reigned 1097-1107)*

With Edgar, Norman influence took a firm hold. A stream of ambitious immigrants, looking for land, power and preferment, began to arrive; encouraged by the king, whose sister Matilda became wife of Henry I of England. It was a time of new developments, stimulated by the energy of the newcomers amd their anxiety to establish themselves firmly. Castles were built, churches and markets founded, and the king's main seat was moved from the religious centre of Dunfermline to the fortress town of Edinburgh.

ALEXANDER I *(born c. 1077, reigned 1107-24)*

The third son of Malcolm and St Margaret had to share power with his brother David, who ruled the south-west in something of a reversion to former practice. He worked hard to strengthen and develop the position of the Church. Scotland had no archbishop, and authority over the Church in Scotland was claimed by the Archbishop of York. The Church was supra-national, and the concept of nationhood scarcely existed, but already tensions and jealousies between the governments of Scotland and England were emerging. The Church in Scotland was both wealthier and better organised than the state at this time, and control of it by a foreign prelate was felt to be intolerable.

DAVID I *(born c. 1080, reigned 1124-53)*
Through his English wife, David became a feudal magnate in England, one of the great men in the inter-related Norman network that by now stretched from the reedy fields of Edinburgh to the orange groves of Palermo. Like his predecessors, he had to deal with uprisings in the North; he too quelled them and gave the forfeited lands and titles to Norman adventurers. He was an exceptionally pious king and founded new dioceses and

Coin of David I

religious houses, such as the great abbeys of Kelso and Jedburgh. Looking enviously at the wealth of these foundations, a Stewart successor called David "a sore saint for the crown". But in his long reign, the rudiments of a government were also set up, and economic growth was encouraged by the first Scottish coinage.

MALCOLM IV *(born 1141, reigned 1153-65)*

David's only son Henry, Earl of Northumberland, died before his father, and the kingship passed to the eldest grandson; primogeniture (the inheritance of the first-born) was now accepted, though not without contest. Malcolm was only eleven, and had plenty of trouble from the Gaelic provinces, especially in the West, where the Lords of the Isles were kings in all but name. But he had a powerful friend in his kinsman Henry II of England, to whom he paid homage. Malcolm was called "the Maiden", a reference to his youth and chastity rather than to effeminacy.

WILLIAM I *(born 1143, reigned 1165-1214)*

Malcolm died young, and his brother reigned after him for almost fifty years. William, named "the Lion" after his death (perhaps because at this time the lion became the Scottish royal emblem) attempted to conquer the northern counties of England. But Henry II captured him at Alnwick in Northumberland in 1174 and compelled William to sign the

Queen Margaret's chapel in Edinburgh Castle

Treaty of Falaise, making Scotland in effect a sub-kingdom of England. The Scottish Church was declared subordinate to the English, and English troops garrisoned four strategic castles, including Edinburgh and Stirling.

This might have meant the beginning of the end for the young kingdom. But the Church fought fiercely for its independence and in 1189 succeeded in making itself directly answerable to the Pope in Rome. And when Henry II died, his successor, the crusading Richard I, was happy to annul the fatal treaty for the sum of 10,000 marks to help finance his holy war against the Saracens. The integrity of the Scottish kingdom was restored.

ALEXANDER II *(born 1198, reigned 1214-49)*

Continuing the policy of his predecessors, Alexander carried on the unsuccessful struggle to gain control of Cumberland, Westmorland and Northumberland. Eventually, he made peace with Henry III and, again like his predecessors, found a queen in England: Henry's sister Joan. He then turned his attention north and west, and set out to enforce his rule as far away as Caithness, where the earls were unaccustomed to royal interference; and to gain the Hebrides, still held by Norway. He died on campaign on the island of Kerrera, in Oban Bay.

ALEXANDER III *(born 1241, reigned 1249-86)*

The only son of Alexander II and his French second wife, Marie de Couci; he was crowned at the age of seven at Scone, on the mysterious Stone of Destiny (despite the degree of "Normanisation", the Celtic traditions remained strong, and the Scottish kings took pride in a lineage that reached further back in time than the House of Plantagenet).

Alexander became a formidable king whose name is still linked with a Scottish golden age. In his reign the Hebrides were

acquired by a combination of battle, politics and cash after the death of Haakon IV of Norway. In a new era of friendship, Alexander's daughter married Eric II of Norway. The last two decades of the reign were fairly peaceful and prosperous, though Scotland continued to have a reputation beyond its borders for poverty, rough manners and lawlessness. And like other golden ages, this one preceded a time of tragedy and turmoil. In 1286 Alexander's horse stumbled and threw him over a cliff near Kinghorn in Fife.

Under the Celtic kings Scotland had established her frontiers (except for the Orkneys and Shetland), but the years of struggle were about to begin.

MARGARET (born 1283, reigned 1286-90)
Alexander III's children had died before him. His nearest heir was the three-year-old "Maid of Norway", his grand-daughter. Great plans were made for this child, who was intended to marry the future Edward II of England, but she died in Orkney, on her way to be crowned.

Thirteen claimants came forward for the throne. There was a period of confusion and alarm, with civil war seeming inevitable, and Edward I of England was presented with a splendid opportunity to become the arbiter of the various claims.

Candidates for the Scottish throne swear homage to the English King Edward

3

The Contested Throne and the Interregnum

JOHN BALLIOL *(born c. 1250, reigned 1292-96, died c. 1313)*
There were no successors to the Celtic kings through the male
line. But in England David, Earl of Huntingdon and grandson of
King David I, had had three daughters. Now the main con-
tenders for the throne were descendants of these daughters:
John Balliol was grandson of the eldest, and Robert Bruce, Earl
of Annandale, son of the second. Bruce was a generation closer
to royalty, but Balliol was descended from the eldest. On this
ground of primogeniture Edward selected Balliol. All the candidates had been compelled to swear homage to the King of
England; and Balliol assumed the kingship as Edward's feudal
vassal.

This was Scotland's most inglorious king, despised by his
people and posterity as "Toom Tabard" (a royal cloak with noth-
ing inside it). Even he finally made resistance to the overbearing
Edward, and was humiliated, imprisoned and exiled for his

pains. It was at this time that Edward had the Stone of Destiny removed from Scone to Westminster Abbey.

THE INTERREGNUM *(1296-1306)*

Scotland was now ruled as if it were a conquered land under military occupation. At this time arose the first great national hero, William Wallace, whose campaign of resistance went on until he was betrayed and handed over to the English in 1304. The savagery of his execution was never forgotten. Leadership in the fight for independence then was claimed by Robert Bruce,

---

The Stone of Destiny had been brought by the Scots from Ireland, first to Iona, then to Scone when that Pictish meeting-place became the coronation site for Kings of Scots. Its origins were already lost in myth; it was said to have been Jacob's pillow in the desert. Other stones or boulders, including the one to be seen at Dunollie Castle, near Oban, are known to have been used in the inauguration of Celtic kings, but none rivalled the mystic prestige of this one. Efforts were made to have it returned to Scotland in 1328, but were frustrated by rioting Londoners. In 1950 a further attempt also ended in failure. In 1996 it was at last returned to Scotland, where it now rests with the "Honours" of Scotland (see page 49) in Edinburgh Castle.

The Stone of Destiny

grandson of the Earl of Annandale and so a remote descendant of the kings. Unlike Wallace, he was not seeking a restoration of Balliol: he was determined to gain the crown for himself. In 1306 he slew a rival, Balliol's nephew John Comyn, in church at Dumfries. A month later he was crowned by the Countess of Buchan (representative, as a MacDuff, of the old Celtic nobility) in front of a few people, at Scone.

Statue of Robert Bruce

4

The Bruces

ROBERT I *(born 1274, reigned 1306-29)*

Excommunicated and by no means universally accepted, Bruce still had a long way to go. He was a king in hiding, and the celebrated spider legend, attesting to his perseverance, dates from this time. The death of the grim Edward I in 1307 was a fortunate event, but Bruce's ambition, determination and leadership were tested to the full in the next seven years of guerrilla warfare. By 1314 he was master of all Scotland except for Stirling Castle. It was to relieve the English garrison there, and reinstate English hegemony, that Edward II brought his vast army North in 1314, only to suffer the decisive defeat at Bannockburn.

Many years passed before Bruce was freed from excommunication and his claim to the kingship accepted by the Pope - arbiter of such matters in an age when kings were believed to be divinely appointed - and by the English government. But when he died, without achieving his ambition to fight on crusade

Bruce's wanderings in 1307 are not clearly recorded. Some accounts claim he left the country entirely and fled briefly to Norway. But most historians agree that he strayed along the west coast and among the islands. The spider story recounts how, hiding alone in a cave, perhaps in Galloway or on Rathlin Island off the north Irish coast, he watched the efforts of a spider, dangling on its thread, as it tried unsuccessfully to swing itself on to the cave wall. After many tries, it finally succeeded . The fugitive monarch, at the lowest point of his fortunes, took heart from the spider's example. Soon his own efforts began to show some success. The long climb to the mastery of the kingdom was under way.

against the Moors in Spain, he passed on a kingdom that was unitedly and consciously Scottish as never before.

DAVID II *(born 1324, reigned 1329-71)*

The son of Bruce's second marriage, David was another child-king, five years old when he acceded. There was trouble from the Balliols, and Edward, son of the disastrous John, had himself crowned at Scone, but as a puppet of Edward III of England. In 1334, David and his Queen Joanna (daughter of Edward II) were sent to France for safety, while Andrew Murray as Guardian of the Kingdom maintained a guerrilla campaign against Balliol's attempt to rule.

David was able to return in 1341. He invaded England five years later, was taken prisoner and remained in captivity for eleven years. During this period Robert the Steward, son of David's half-sister Marjorie, supervised affairs in a grisly time of

David II fled to France as a child

plague, lawlessness and Border strife. David made his second return in 1357, at the price of a vast ransom to be paid over ten years, and thereafter concentrated on ruling his run-down and unsettled kingdom.

The Scottish royal arms

5

The House of Stewart

Surnames in the fourteenth century were not the fixed things they are today, and men were often known by their functions, their nicknames or, in the Gaelic/Norse areas, as the sons of their fathers. Among the officers of the court since the reign of David I was the High Steward, and Robert I's daughter Marjorie married Walter the Steward. David II died childless, and his nearest heir, the son of Marjorie and Walter, became king at the age of fifty-five. Thus from the Stewards emerged the Stewart dynasty which would eventually reign over Scotland, England and Ireland.

ROBERT II *(born 1316, reigned 1371-90)*
Previous kings of Scotland had maintained strong diplomatic links with France, as a counterbalance to the might of England, but under Robert II the "auld alliance" emerged in full vigour,

and French troops landed in Scotland to help against English attack. When not fighting the English, the Scottish barons fought among themselves: it was a troubled and unruly period. Robert was a weak king; he knew himself to be a jumped-up baron and had neither the ability nor the will to impose his authority.

ROBERT III *(born c. 1337, reigned 1390-1406)*

His baptismal name was John, but memory of John Balliol was too recent, and as king he took the more illustrious name of

Robert III's brother, "the Wolf of Badenoch", burned Elgin Cathedral

Robert. But he was another weak and ineffective ruler. His own family were behaving like brigands: his brother Alexander, "the Wolf of Badenoch", burned Elgin Cathedral and committed many other acts of banditry in the Highlands. Robert's sixteen-year reign continued the chronicle of plagues, battles, raids and counter-raids. His depressive nature seems to foreshadow such distant descendants as the Old Pretender. Just before his death he was given the news that his 11-year-old son, James, who had been sent to France for security, had been captured at sea by the English. On his deathbed he asked to be buried on a dungheap.

JAMES I *(born 1394, reigned 1406-37)*

It was not until James was nearly thirty that he was able to return to his kingdom. His uncle, the Duke of Albany, ruled, or presided over the unruliness of the other lords. James, short, stout, energetic and impatient, set out to change all that. He was a man of culture, action and ideas, the author of *The Kingis Quair* (King's Book), a love-poem to his English bride, Joan Beaufort. With a clear view of what a king was supposed to do, he made efforts to discipline the lawless nobility, and set out to improve the king's position by encouraging commerce (for taxes) and military strength, forbidding football in favour of archery practice. But he inevitably made powerful enemies, and a group of conspirators stabbed him to death one night as he tried to hide in the stinking outfall of the privy in the Blackfriars' house in Perth.

His reign set a pattern for the Stewart kings to follow him: coming to the throne as children, emerging from minority to assert themselves while still in their teens. With limited resources they had to establish control over powerful and unscrupulous barons. Each reign was a struggle to maintain the balance of power.

JAMES II *(born 1430, reigned 1437-60)*

One of James I's killers, the Earl of Atholl, was a claimant to the throne, but tradition held firm. He was gruesomely crowned with a red-hot iron, then beheaded, and James's six-year-old son was crowned king - the first to be crowned in Edinburgh and not at Scone. As a child he endured a chaotic life as the prisoner of different factions and strong-men, but as a young man asserted his own authority and became himself the prime mover of events. Nicknamed "James of the Fiery Face" from a red birth-mark, he matched any of his barons in ruthlessness. With his own dagger he stabbed the Earl of Douglas in Stirling Castle, and destroyed the power of the "Black Douglases", who controlled the Border and much of the south. James II was well-embarked on a strong-handed reign, maintaining the policies begun by his father, when he was killed by an exploding cannon while trying to retrieve Roxburgh Castle from the English.

The young king was brought up in the life-style of a lord: instructed in the code of chivalry, trained to hunt and joust as well as to read and write. The courtly ways developed in the great duchies and kingdoms of Europe were followed as far as the resources of the royal money-chest could stretch. From earliest youth he would know his own significance. He would be taught the fundamentals of Scotland's situation, its relations with Ireland, England, France, the North Sea states. Surrounded by tutors and advisers, some of them concerned for his and the country's welfare, others only for their own advantage, he had to learn judgement. But above all, he had to impose himself, or become the prisoner of events.

St Magnus Cathedral, Kirkwall, Orkney (founded in 1138).
Orkney and Shetland became part of Scotland in the reign of James III.

JAMES III *(born 1452, reigned 1460-88)*

Here was yet another boy-king, and also destined for a violent death. It was through his marriage with Margaret of Denmark that Scotland gained Orkney and Shetland, pledged against a dowry that was never paid. The politics of the time were profoundly influenced by events in England, where the warring Yorkists and Lancastrians both sought Scottish alliances, and even a great baron like the Lord of the Isles was prepared to see the kingdom broken up in order to secure control of his own dominion. James's personal relations with the barons, including his own two brothers, were hostile; rough types happiest on the jousting field, they despised his intellectual and cultural interests. Unusually among the Stewart kings, he did not succeed in playing them off against each other, and eventually a group of them combined against him. He faced an open rebellion that had seized his own son as its figurehead, was defeated in battle and killed by an unknown hand after it, at the age of thirty-six.

JAMES IV *(born 1472, reigned 1488-1513)*

The fourth James made a marriage with Margaret Tudor, daughter to Henry VII of England. This was to be of profound importance to his great-grandson, James VI. James wore an iron chain as a public penance for his involuntary part in his father's death. He was an ardent pilgrim, making regular visits to such shrines as St Duthac's in Tain, in the Highlands. But he was far from being the contemplative type. Eager, affable, popular, he ranged the country as none of its kings had done before. He spoke Gaelic, and managed to achieve somewhat more control in the Highlands and Islands. Even in the disturbed years of the first Jameses, Scotland had seen the foundation of universities and the growth of a national literature based on English (Gaelic culture and its oral tradition continued to flourish, unheeded outside the Highlands); now the new learning took great steps forward. But James also looked abroad and wanted to play a part in

James IV was killed at Flodden

European diplomacy and war. He amassed armaments, especially ships, far beyond what the country could afford. When Henry VIII and Louis XII of France went to war, James took a great army south to support the French. Just over the Border, at Flodden, he was shatteringly defeated, and fell fighting on the battlefield.

JAMES V *(born 1512, reigned 1513-42)*
The new king was one year old. His English mother was briefly regent, then the Duke of Albany took over and brought the boy up under the aegis of the French alliance. When James was about 12, his mother regained control of the government, but the king was in the hands of the "Red Douglases" under the Earl of Angus until 1528, when he escaped from their clutches and set about becoming master of the kingdom. Seeking a bride with a rich dowry, he married first Madeleine, daughter of the French king Francis I, who died almost immediately, then another Frenchwoman, Mary of Guise.

James V ruled vigorously and with an eye to enlarging the royal treasure chest, which rankled both with the nobles and with the Church, which supplied most of the money. During his reign there were further improvements in the operation of the law. With a taste for the architectural styles of the time, he extended his father's palaces at Stirling, Falkland and Linlithgow. He was also celebrated for his incognito excursions by night and had numerous children outside his marriage. The Pope, anxious to hold Scotland's loyalty during his struggles with Henry VIII of England, gladly agreed to bestow high church rank and benefices on these infants. Always anti-English in his outlook, James eventually antagonised Henry to the point where an English army was sent to invade, and defeated the Scots in the ramshackle battle of Solway Moss. James, exhausted and depressed, died shortly afterwards in Falkland Palace. He was still a young man: his daughter and heir was only a few days old.

MARY *(born 1542, reigned 1542-67, executed 1587)*
She is perhaps the most famous of all Scotland's monarchs, although her reign was a disaster for herself and the country. Of all the child-heirs she was the youngest; throughout her childhood her mother, the resolute Mary of Guise, was Regent, and struggled to maintain the French connection against the pro-English faction, which was growing in strength as Protestantism took hold. But in 1560, the year of Mary of Guise's death, a Protestant government, with English support, sent her French troops and advisors home. Mary Queen of Scots' early years were eventful.

At the age of six she was sent to France; still as a child she was wedded to the French heir, Louis, and actually reigned with him as Queen of France (he was titular King of Scotland). But he died in 1561, and as a nineteen-year-old widow she came home

Stirling Castle was extended during the reign of James V

to meet the rigours of the climate, the domestic arrangements and the Protestant Reformers.

Seven years later she fled to England, to whose crown she had never given up her claim (in the eyes of Catholics, Elizabeth I of England was illegitimate and had no right to the throne). It was not Mary's Catholicism that had ruined her, but her inept rule and her choice of men. Mary had defended herself and her religion staunchly in her debates with the reformer John Knox, but she was happier on hunting trips in the hills than in the violent

Mary Queen of Scots

and changeable jungle of Scottish politics. First she had married Lord Darnley, an ambitious playboy of royal blood, and soon tired of him. His jealousy helped provoke the lurid murder of Mary's secretary, perhaps lover, David Riccio. But Mary could not escape implication in the murder of Darnley himself, found strangled in the garden of his blazing house. Her third husband, the Earl of Bothwell, was an unscrupulous Border warlord.

The increasingly violent demands for Protestant reform opened up wide divisions in the country, but the throne remained the one unifying influence. However, when Mary and Darnley produced a son, she was no longer vital: the succession was provided for. The baby boy became the ward of the

Elizabeth was Queen of England; Philip was King of Spain. But the Scottish monarch was King, or Queen, of Scots. This difference in style goes back to the four "Dark Age" kingdoms. The Scots of Dalriada were one tribal group and their king was their chief. In Latin he was *Rex Scottorum*. The Scots absorbed the Picts and became the largest group in the country. So there was a King of Scots before there was a Scotland, and the ancient usage was never dropped even when Scotland became a unified nation. Had things gone differently in the ninth century, she might have been Mary, Queen of Picts, and the country Pictland.

James VI

Protestant party, and eventually Mary's enemies combined in rebellion: she was defeated, imprisoned, forced to abdicate, escaped, and fled humiliatingly to sanctuary with her great rival, Elizabeth.

She remained a frustrated captive for nineteen years. Once it seemed she might have been Queen of Scotland, England, Ireland and France. Now she fretted, plotted, was drawn into the intrigues of others. Eventually the English executed her for treason, in 1587. Since then, the torrent of words has never ceased: plays, operas, novels, biographies. The elements of light and dark in her life - glamour and scandal, courage without judgement, good fortune and bad - are endlessly explorable. Failure raises more questions than success.

JAMES VI *(born 1566, reigned 1567-1625)*

The first Stewart kings, conscious of their non-royal origins, were hesitant monarchs. The ninth had no such anxieties. He wrote two books on kingship and fostered the notion that a king had a God-given right to rule. Because of his mother's abdication, he too was a child-king and learned the hard way how to play off the bitter and violent factions in the country and even in his own household. He was well educated in the style of the time, having had Latin thrashed into him by the eminent scholar, George Buchanan.

James had much to look forward to if he could survive: he

The Authorised, or "King James" version of the Bible

was the nearest heir to the childless Elizabeth I of England, as a result of the marriage between James IV and Margaret Tudor. He took good care not to offend Elizabeth or her government, making only a token protest even when his mother was executed. But James VI was in any case perhaps the most successful Stuart king (they had adopted the French spelling of the name).

His autocratic aims were cloaked in humour, informality, and a wide range of interests. He had a view on everything: he wrote a "Counterblast Against Tobacco", without result, but his belief in witchcraft caused the persecution and death of many helpless old women. Perhaps the greatest achievement of his reign was the publication of the Authorised or "King James" Version of the Bible. The width of his interests and his readiness to make a statement earned him the description "the wisest fool in Christendom", which has has rather unfairly dogged his reputation. His affection for male favourites caused whispers of homosexuality, although he and his queen, Anne of Denmark, also produced eight children.

In 1603, on the death of Elizabeth I of England, James received the long-anticipated call from London, and set off with, among other things, his golf-clubs. Despite a promise to return often, he came back to Scotland only once in the next 22 years, governing at long range through a Privy Council. James was keen on the political union of "Great Britain", but Scotland was to remain a separate state for another century.

The Palace of Dunfermline, birthplace of Charles I

6

The Dual Kingdom

CHARLES I *(born 1600, reigned 1625-49)*
Scotland was not to see much more of her kings, except when
they needed her help to survive. Charles I, born in Dunfermline,
waited seven years before he came to Edinburgh to be crowned.
His religious policy, with its bishops and its "Popish" liturgy, was
widely disliked in Scotland and in 1638 the National Covenant
was set up. It offered Charles its loyalty but also demanded a free
parliament and general assembly of the Church: intolerable to
the imperious Charles, who shared his father's belief in the
divine right of kings. He sent an army to command obedience;
it was beaten and the Scots occupied Newcastle. Charles had to
make concessions. He came a second time to Edinburgh in
1641, in the hope of keeping Scotland loyal as civil war loomed
in England. But the Covenanters, firmly in charge, sided with
the London Parliament. In 1647 the defeated Charles gave himself up to the Scottish army at Newark in England; they kept him

for seven months, then handed him over to the army of the English Parliament. He was beheaded in London in January 1649, conducting himself with impressive dignity to the last.

CHARLES II *(born 1630, reigned 1649-51, 1660-85)*

His son was promptly proclaimed king in Edinburgh, where they had not forgotten where the Stuarts came from. Charles II landed in Scotland in 1650 and clung on until 1651, when he was crowned at Scone. On invading England later that year, he was routed by Cromwell at Worcester and fled to France.

For nine years Cromwell ruled Scotland much as Edward I had done. His laws and the efficiency of his governor, General Monck, did more to subdue the turbulent barons of Scotland than any of her kings. Monck died in 1660, and Charles II was soon called back to England. Charles had seen enough of Scotland to satisfy him already; though he had once promised to uphold the Covenant, he said that Presbyterianism "was no religion for a gentleman". The Duke of Lauderdale implemented his policies for most of the reign. Religious warfare in the south-west, which was a stronghold of extreme Covenanters, disfigured the time.

In his humour, affability and intellectual curiosity Charles II took after his grandfather James VI, though Scotland had no chance to appreciate his personal qualities after 1651. In his brother, as in his father, the less attractive and less successful aspects of the Stuarts were displayed - imperiousness, inflexibility and fatalistic gloom.

The "Honours" of Scotland - crown, sword of state and sceptre - are still be seen in Edinburgh Castle. Charles II was crowned with this crown, made in Edinburgh for James IV, but after his coronation the "Honours" disappeared. Between 1650 and 1658 they were kept hidden from the Cromwell regime, first in Dunottar Castle, near Stonehaven, then in the manse of nearby Kinneff, from where they were moved to the church there, and kept under the floorboards. In 1707, year of the Union of the Parliaments, they were walled up in Edinburgh Castle and half-forgotten, to be "re-discovered" after more than a century by Sir Walter Scott and others, in 1818.

JAMES VII and II *(born 1633, reigned 1685-88, died 1701)*

On Charles' death with numerous children but none legitimate, his brother became king at the age of 52. As Duke of York he had already been his brother's manager of Scottish affairs for several years, placing his own men in power. James was an ardent Roman Catholic, ruling over two nations who had fought bloody wars in the Protestant cause. Trouble was inevitable. His short reign was marked in Scotland by the Earl of Argyll's failed rebellion in the west, and by intensified warfare in the south-west, the long-remembered "killing time". In 1688, William of Orange landed at Torbay, and James fled, was captured, escaped, and joined his Queen and baby son in France. For the rest of his life he would be "the King over the Water".

WILLIAM *(born 1650, reigned 1688-1702)* and MARY *(Born 1662, reigned 1688-94)*

Scotland had played no part in James's deposition or in the invitation to William of Orange. But he and his joint sovereign, Mary, James VII's daughter, were duly proclaimed in Edinburgh. Theirs had been a dynastic marriage; Mary had wept for a day on hearing what had been arranged for her. Despite the Stuart blood of both (William was a grandson of Charles I), they were widely regarded as usurpers, especially in the Catholic Highlands. John Graham of Claverhouse, or "Bonnie Dundee", the scourge of the Covenanters, fought for the exiled king, win-

King Charles II

ning, but dying in, the Battle of Killiecrankie. With him gone, the Stuart cause had no leader. As before, Scotland was ruled through a Privy Council. It was not a wholly civilised government, financially corrupt and with the Massacre of Glencoe (1690), to answer for. Despite the long-demanded removal of bishops from the Church, it was not a popular reign. When Scotland's commercial interests conflicted with England's,

Why did the Stuart Pretenders not follow in reverse the example of Henry of Navarre, who became a Catholic to win the French throne as Henri IV? A switch of religion would have regained them not one, but three crowns. In such a long-lasting dynasty, it is pointless to look for recurrent characteristics. The early Jameses were ruthless practical politicians. The later Stuarts believed firmly in their God-given right to rule; indeed Charles I died for his own notion of kingship. His descendants had already experienced one Restoration in 1660 - why not another? They knew they had British supporters as well as continental allies. Their attitude may have been arrogant, or stupid, or highly-principled. But a court in exile, sustained by memories, dreams and myths, expected by its allies or paymasters to maintain its historic identity, can lock itself into a pattern of belief and behaviour that is virtually impossible to escape from.

William ignored her, and Scotland gained little from what in England was the "Glorious Revolution".

ANNE *(born 1665, reigned 1702-14)*

William and Mary had no children, and Mary's sister Anne inherited the throne, the second Stuart Queen to rule in her own right. By then the monarch's powers, though always greater in Scotland than in England, were more limited; and in any case Anne was much more prudent and circumspect than her ancestress Mary. She visited Scotland only once, as a teenage girl, never as Queen. Seventeen pregnancies occupied much of her life, but none of her children survived her. In what she hailed as the most glorious achievement of her reign, the Scottish and English Parliaments were united as the Parliament of Great Britain (1707). There was much concern about her successor. James VII and II had died in exile in 1702, and he had a son, whom his supporters saw as the rightful James VIII and III. But the exiled Stuarts remained staunchly Catholic, and anti-Catholic feeling in England was so strong as to make a recall impossible.

Prince Charles Edward, "Bonnie Prince Charlie"

7

The Hanoverian Monarchy

The English government, before the Union, had already sought out a suitable candidate for the throne in a German prince whose mother was a grand-daughter of James VI, and who satisfied the two chief requirements: a drop of Stuart blood in his veins and firm adherence to the Protestant persuasion. So in 1714 began the long line of German Georges. "Wha the de'il hae we gotten for a king, but a wee, wee German lairdie!" sang the Jacobites in derision.

Dissatisfaction with the Union, ancient loyalty, and for many, religious sympathy with the Stuarts, produced the 1715 Rebellion. "James VIII", the Old Pretender, arrived in Scotland for a few wintry weeks, but left when failure was obvious. Although Jacobitism, backed by French money and intrigue, continued to trouble the central government, the landing of James's 25-year-old son, Prince Charles Edward, at Moidart, in the western Highlands, in 1745, came as a surprise. With a

The memorial cairn at Culloden

Highland army he occupied Edinburgh, defeated a government force at Prestonpans and marched into England. But England did not rally to him. He reluctantly retreated to Scotland and into the Highlands again, to the ultimate defeat at Culloden in April 1746. Five months of hiding followed before he escaped to France and a long, undistinguished retirement, signing himself "Carolus Rex" to the end. His younger brother Henry, a cardinal at the Papal court, then assumed the futile title Henry IX.

"Bonnie Prince Charlie" in his youth had taken a bold risk, and through him a tinge of glamour and romance still clings to the lost Stuart cause. He had an illegitimate daughter, to whom he gave the title Duchess of Albany, and she had a son, who died childless in 1854. Though many royal, and non-royal, families, would claim Stuart ancestry, the Stuart dynasty was dead.

8

Hanover to Windsor

Political reform and the development of the modern British state meant a steady reduction of royal power through the later 18th and the 19th centuries. The king, though still influential, no longer determined policy, and the monarch's role became an increasingly ceremonial one.

The only member of the House of Hanover to be much involved with Scotland was the Duke of Cumberland, son of King George II, the victor at Culloden, and known as "Butcher" for his actions afterwards. George I and II were more interested in their German domains, and neither they nor George III throughout his lengthy reign ever set foot in Scotland. The Northern kingdom remained ignored until the famous visit of George IV to Edinburgh in 1822, a public relations exercise masterminded by Sir Walter Scott, which even saw the portly monarch rigged out in a kilt and flesh-pink tights.

A more enduring link between the royal family and Scotland

The Highland Gathering at Braemer

was established with Queen Victoria's purchase of Balmoral; by mid-century the railway could transport her there in ease and comfort. The earnest Queen took great pride in the remote Stuart element of her pedigree and, with the Stuart line safely extinct, was even something of a Jacobite. Scotland became the royal family's summer retreat, to the pleasure of many Scots, whose interest in the royal family increased again when Lady

Elizabeth Bowes-Lyon, daughter of the Earl of Strathmore, married the future King George VI in 1923.

Many Scots were displeased when twentieth-century kings such as Edward VII, Edward VIII and later Queen Elizabeth II were not officially recognised in Scotland, where their predecessors of the same name had never ruled, as Edward I and Edward II, and Elizabeth I. It was as if history had been rewritten by London bureaucrats, making Plantagenets and Tudors rulers of Scotland, and ignoring that long line of Scottish kings, stretch

One curious quirk of the Scottish-English union is that the monarch is still Head of both the English and the Scottish Established Churches, the one Episcopalian, the other Presbyterian. This necessitates a significant change in religious outlook each time the Border is crossed.

ing back into the remote mists of Celtic history, as if they had never been. Yet it was precisely that Scottish ancestry which gave the German-born royal house its claim to reign in the United Kingdom. The union of two countries under one crown can still create controversy, even after some four hundred years.

A Royal Welcome in 1633

King Charles 1 enters Edinburgh to be crowned

At the West Port, his Majestie had ane eloquent speech, making him wellcome, and the keys of the toun offered him by the speaker... As he entered in... Alexander Clerk, provost, in name of the rest, and toun of Edinburgh, made some short speech, and therwith presented to his Majestie ane bason all of gold, estimate to five thousand merks, wherein was shaken out of an embroidered purse ane thousand golden double angells, as ane token of the toun of Edinburgh, their love and humble service... At his entry at the port of the Upper Bow, he had ane third speech. At the West End of the Tolbuith he saw the royal pedegree of the Kings of Scotland, frae Fergus the First, delicately painted; and then had ane fourth speech. At the Mercat Croce he had ane fifth speech, when his Majestie's health was heartilie drunken... At the Tron, Parnassus Hill was curiouslie erected, all grein with birks, where nine prettie boys, representing the nine nymphs or muses, was nymph-like cled; when he had the sixth speech; after the which the speaker delivered to his Majestie ane book. And seventhly, he had ane speech at the Nether Bow. Which haill orations, his Majestie, with great pleasure and delyte, sitting on horseback, as his company did, heard pleasantly, syne rode down the Canongate to his own palace of Holyroodhouse, where he stayed that night.

John Spalding, Historie of the Troubles